W9-CNU-679

The Let's Talk Library™

Let's Talk About When You Have Trouble Going to Sleep

Susan Kent

The Rosen Publishing Group's
PowerKids Press™
New York

To Larry Swann, for everything.

Published in 2000 by The Rosen Publishing Group, Inc.
29 East 21st Street, New York, NY 10010

First Edition

Book design: Erin McKenna

Photo Credits: pp. 4, 8, 15 by Emily Moody, p. 7 by John Bentham, p. 11 © Scott Barrow/ International Stock, pp. 12, 20 © George Ancona/ International Stock, pp. 16, 19 by Seth Dinnerman.

Kent, Susan, 1942—
    Let's talk about when you have trouble going to sleep / by Susan Kent.
        p.   cm.— (The Let's talk library)
    Includes index.
    Summary: Discusses the importance of sleep, the effects of not getting enough sleep, and routines to ease the process of bedtime.
    ISBN 0-8239-5424-2 (lib. bdg.)
    1. Sleep—Juvenile literature. 2. Children—Sleep—Juvenile literature. [1. Sleep. 2. Bedtime.] I. Title.
II. Series.
RA786.K44 1999
618.92'8498—dc21   98-50163
                                                                                CIP
                                                                                AC

Manufactured in the United States of America

Table of Contents

Jonah

Jonah is having a bad day at school. He keeps bumping into desks and chairs. He has trouble paying attention to his teacher. She calls on him three times before he hears her. In gym class, he cannot run fast or respond quickly. He even misses the ball when it is thrown right to him. When his best friend, Anthony, asks what is wrong, Jonah says, "Nothing." Something is the matter, though. Jonah didn't get enough sleep last night.

◄ *Jonah doesn't feel well when he hasn't had enough sleep. He finds it hard to stay awake in school.*

What Happens When You Sleep?

When you sleep, you are **unconscious**. You don't know what is going on around you. Your breathing and heartbeat slow down. Your **muscles**, like the ones in your arms and legs, are limp. Your **temperature** is lower than when you are awake. That is why you usually need a cover when you sleep.

You probably do not lie still when you sleep. You usually move from side to side. If your foot is tickled, you pull it away. When you wake up, though, you won't remember moving.

When your muscles relax and your breathing slows, your body is getting the rest it needs to be ready for the next day. ▶

When You Don't Sleep Well

When you don't get enough sleep, like Jonah, you find it hard to think and to **concentrate**. You feel very tired, and your body feels heavy. It is hard to keep your eyes open, and your eyelids feel dry. You cannot get comfortable. Every position you try in your chair feels worse than the last. You wish you could be lying down. On top of all this, you are probably **irritable**. You are cranky even with your friends.

◄ *This boy did not have a good night's sleep. He is too tired to concentrate on his homework.*

What Keeps You Awake?

Many things can keep you awake. You might have trouble sleeping when you are excited or when you are scared, like after you watch a horror show on television. Maybe you are worried about a test in school or sad because your mom or dad is leaving on a business trip. Sometimes when you are active, like after playing basketball, you may toss and turn at night. All of these different feelings can cause trouble sleeping.

To fall asleep, you need to calm down and **relax**.

There are lots of reasons why people have trouble sleeping. ▶
It might be because of something you've seen on television.

Anika

A huge dog with yellow eyes, sharp teeth, and a long wet tongue is chasing Anika. As it is getting closer, she cries, "Help!" and wakes up.

She goes into her parents' room and tells them about her nightmare. Her mommy and daddy hug her and tell her she is safe. When she calms down, they take her back to her bed and tuck her in. Her mommy hums a lullaby. This time, Anika sleeps through the night.

◀ *After Anika has a bad dream, her mom stays with her for a while until she falls back asleep.*

Nightmares

Everyone has nightmares. You might have them when you are sick or when you have a fever. They might happen if you have an argument with a friend or if the class bully teases you. If you have an operation or are in a car accident, you might have nightmares afterward. Sad events like losing a pet, or anything else that upsets you, can give you bad dreams. Nightmares are not fun, but they are a common part of life and sometimes help you to work out something that is bothering you.

Some kids have nightmares when they are sick with a fever. ▶

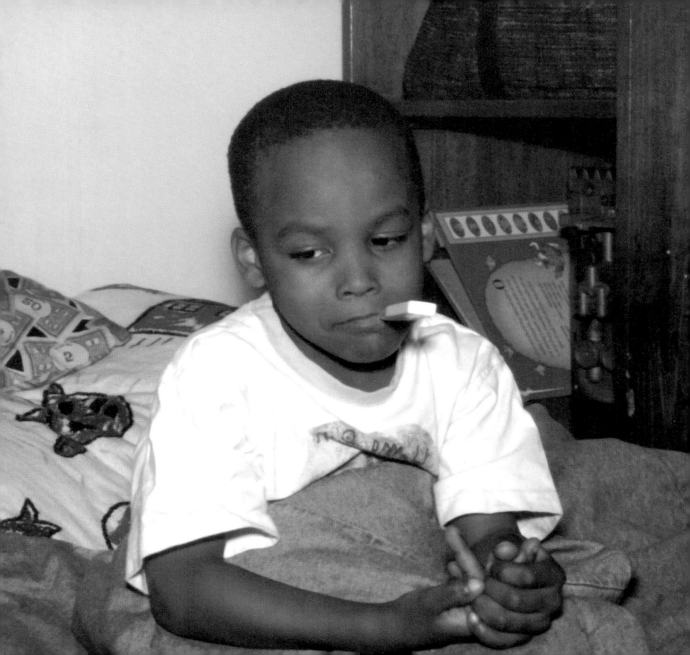

How Long Should You Sleep?

At different ages, you need different amounts of sleep. Babies usually sleep more than 16 hours. You probably need about 10 or 11 hours a night, while your parents need only 6 to 9 hours. However, each person is different. Some people need more sleep and some need less.

Sometimes you sleep longer if you have been very active. After a full day at an amusement park, you might sleep late the next morning. After a rainy day spent reading, however, you might wake up early.

If you have spent the day reading in bed, you might not ◀ *need as much sleep as you usually do when you are very active and busy.*

How to Fall Asleep

Falling asleep is easiest if you have a bedtime **routine**. Try to do the same things each night. Unless there is a special reason to stay up, always go to bed at the same time. Exercise during the day helps you sleep at night, but right before bed it can keep you awake. Try reading or listening to calm music to help you fall asleep. A comfortable bed always helps, and some people sleep better with a night-light.

This girl listens to soft music as she falls asleep. ▶

Kelly and Keith

It is time for Kelly and Keith to go to bed. After a glass of milk and some cookies, they have warm baths and brush their teeth. They each pick out a story for their dad to read. After the stories, their mom turns out the light and sings their favorite lullabies. Kelly and Keith both get hugs and kisses from Mom and Dad. They snuggle under their blankets with their stuffed bears. They fall asleep with the moon shining in their window.

◀ *These children brush their teeth before going to bed. It's a good idea to have a bedtime routine.*

Good Morning!

After a good night's sleep, you wake up feeling great. Your eyes are bright. You feel active and full of energy. You are ready to get out of bed and start the day.

Whatever you do, you will be able to pay attention and do your best. You will be in a good mood, so you can have lots of fun with your friends.

Have a wonderful day!

Glossary

concentrate (KAHN-sin-trayt) To focus your thoughts and attention on something.

irritable (EER-ih-tuh-bul) Tense, cranky, or grouchy.

muscles (MUH-sulz) Parts of the body underneath the skin that can be tightened or loosened to make the body move.

relax (ree-LAKS) To feel loose, or to let go of tension, stiffness, or worry.

routine (ROO-teen) Something you do over and over in the same way.

temperature (TEHM-per-ah-chur) How hot or cold something is, like the human body.

unconscious (un-KAHN-shus) Not aware of what is going on around you.

Index